Great Works Instructional Guides for Literature

Are You My Mother?

A guide for the book by P. D. Eastman
Great Works Author: Jodene Smith, M.A.

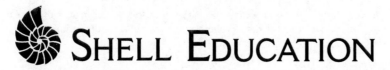

SHELL EDUCATION

Image Credits

Julie C. Wagner Shutterstock (cover); Timothy J. Bradley (interior art)

Standards

© 2007 Teachers of English to Speakers of Other Languages, Inc. (TESOL)
© 2007 Board of Regents of the University of Wisconsin System. World-Class Instructional Design and Assessment (WIDA)
© Copyright 2010. National Governors Association Center for Best Practices and Council of Chief State School Officers.
All rights reserved.

Shell Education

5301 Oceanus Drive
Huntington Beach, CA 92649-1030
http://www.shelleducation.com
ISBN 978-1-4258-8963-0
© 2014 Shell Educational Publishing, Inc.

Table of contents

How to Use This Literature Guide

Today's standards demand rigor and relevance in the reading of complex texts. The units in this series guide teachers in a rich and deep exploration of worthwhile works of literature for classroom study. The most rigorous instruction can also be interesting and engaging!

Many current strategies for effective literacy instruction have been incorporated into these instructional guides for literature. Throughout the units, text-dependent questions are used to determine comprehension of the book as well as student interpretation of the vocabulary words. The books chosen for the series are complex and are exemplars of carefully crafted works of literature. Close reading is used throughout the units to guide students toward revisiting the text and using textual evidence to respond to prompts orally and in writing. Students must analyze the story elements in multiple assignments for each section of the book. All of these strategies work together to rigorously guide students through their study of literature.

The next few pages describe how to use this guide for a purposeful and meaningful literature study. Each section of this guide is set up in the same way to make it easier for you to implement the instruction in your classroom.

Theme Thoughts

The great works of literature used throughout this series have important themes that have been relevant to people for many years. Many of the themes will be discussed during the various sections of this instructional guide. However, it would also benefit students to have independent time to think about the key themes of the book.

Before students begin reading, have them complete the *Pre-Reading Theme Thoughts* (page 13). This graphic organizer will allow students to think about the themes outside the context of the story. They'll have the opportunity to evaluate statements based on important themes and defend their opinions. Be sure to keep students' papers for comparison to the *Post-Reading Theme Thoughts* (page 59). This graphic organizer is similar to the pre-reading activity. However, this time, students will be answering the questions from the point of view of one of the characters in the book. They have to think about how the character would feel about each statement and defend their thoughts. To conclude the activity, have students compare what they thought about the themes before they read the book to what the characters discovered during the story.

How to Use This Literature Guide (cont.)

Vocabulary

Each teacher reference vocabulary overview page has definitions and sentences about how key vocabulary words are used in the section. These words should be introduced and discussed with students. Students will use these words in different activities throughout the book.

On some of the vocabulary student pages, students are asked to answer text-related questions about vocabulary words from the sections. The following question stems will help you create your own vocabulary questions if you'd like to extend the discussion.

- How does this word describe _____'s character?
- How does this word connect to the problem in this story?
- How does this word help you understand the setting?
- Tell me how this word connects to the main idea of this story.
- What visual pictures does this word bring to your mind?
- Why do you think the author used this word?

At times, you may find that more work with the words will help students understand their meanings and importance. These quick vocabulary activities are a good way to further study the words.

- Students can play vocabulary concentration. Make one set of cards that have the words on them and another set with the definitions. Then, have students lay them out on the table and play concentration. The goal of the game is to match vocabulary words with their definitions. For early readers or English language learners, the two sets of cards could be the words and pictures of the words.
- Students can create word journal entries about the words. Students choose words they think are important and then describe why they think each word is important within the book. Early readers or English language learners could instead draw pictures about the words in a journal.
- Students can create puppets and use them to act out the vocabulary words from the stories. Artwork of the characters is provided on pages 62–64. Students can use these images to retell the stories using the vocabulary words. Students may also enjoy telling their own character-driven stories using vocabulary words from the original stories.

How to Use This Literature Guide (cont.)

Analyzing the Literature

After you have read each section with students, hold a small-group or whole-class discussion. Provided on the teacher reference page for each section are leveled questions. The questions are written at two levels of complexity to allow you to decide which questions best meet the needs of your students. The Level 1 questions are typically less abstract than the Level 2 questions. These questions are focused on the various story elements, such as character, setting, and plot. Be sure to add further questions as your students discuss what they've read. For each question, a few key points are provided for your reference as you discuss the book with students.

Reader Response

In today's classrooms, there are often great readers who are below average writers. So much time and energy is spent in classrooms getting students to read on grade level that little time is left to focus on writing skills. To help teachers include more writing in their daily literacy instruction, each section of this guide has a literature-based reader response prompt. Each of the three genres of writing is used in the reader responses within this guide: narrative, informative/explanatory, and opinion. Before students write, you may want to allow them time to draw pictures related to the topic. Book-themed writing paper is provided on page 70 if your students need more space to write.

Guided Close Reading

Within each section of this guide, it is suggested that you closely reread a portion of the text with your students. Page numbers are given, but since some versions of the books may have different page numbers, the sections to be reread are described by location as well. After rereading the section, there are a few text-dependent questions to be answered by students. Working space has been provided to help students prepare for the group discussion. They should record their thoughts and ideas on the activity page and refer to it during your discussion. If your students are working above grade level, you may want to encourage them to respond to the questions in complete sentences.

Encourage students to read one question at a time and then go back to the text and discover the answer. Work with students to ensure that they use the text to determine their answers rather than making unsupported inferences. Suggested answers are provided in the answer key.

#40000—Instructional Guide: Are You My Mother?   © Shell Education

How to Use This Literature Guide (cont.)

Guided Close Reading (cont.)

The generic open-ended stems below can be used to write your own text-dependent questions if you would like to give students more practice.

- What words in the story support . . . ?
- What text helps you understand . . . ?
- Use the book to tell why _____ happens.
- Based on the events in the story, . . . ?
- Show me the part in the text that supports . . . .
- Use the text to tell why . . . .

Making Connections

The activities in this section help students make cross-curricular connections to mathematics, science, social studies, fine arts, or other curricular areas. These activities require higher-order thinking skills from students but also allow for creative thinking.

Language Learning

A special section has been set aside to connect the literature to language conventions. Through these activities, students will have opportunities to practice the conventions of standard English grammar, usage, capitalization, and punctuation.

Story Elements

It is important to spend time discussing what the common story elements are in literature. Understanding the characters, setting, plot, and theme can increase students' comprehension and appreciation of the story. If teachers begin discussing these elements in early childhood, students will more likely internalize the concepts and look for the elements in their independent reading. Another very important reason for focusing on the story elements is that students will be better writers if they think about how the stories they read are constructed.

In the story elements activities, students are asked to create work related to the characters, setting, or plot. Consider having students complete only one of these activities. If you give students a choice on this assignment, each student can decide to complete the activity that most appeals to him or her. Different intelligences are used so that the activities are diverse and interesting to all students.

How to Use This Literature Guide (cont.)

Culminating Activity

At the end of this instructional guide is a creative culminating activity that allows students the opportunity to share what they've learned from reading the book. This activity is open ended so that students can push themselves to create their own great works within your language arts classroom.

Comprehension Assessment

The questions in this section require students to think about the book they've read as well as the words that were used in the book. Some questions are tied to quotations from the book to engage students and require them to think about the text as they answer the questions.

Response to Literature

Finally, students are asked to respond to the literature by drawing pictures and writing about the characters and stories. A suggested rubric is provided for teacher reference.

Correlation to the Standards

Shell Education is committed to producing educational materials that are research and standards based. As part of this effort, we have correlated all of our products to the academic standards of all 50 states, the District of Columbia, the Department of Defense Dependents Schools, and all Canadian provinces.

Purpose and Intent of Standards

Standards are designed to focus instruction and guide adoption of curricula. Standards are statements that describe the criteria necessary for students to meet specific academic goals. They define the knowledge, skills, and content students should acquire at each level. Standards are also used to develop standardized tests to evaluate students' academic progress. Teachers are required to demonstrate how their lessons meet standards. Standards are used in the development of all of our products, so educators can be assured they meet high academic standards.

How To Find Standards Correlations

To print a customized correlation report of this product for your state, visit our website at http://www.shelleducation.com and follow the online directions. If you require assistance in printing correlation reports, please contact our Customer Service Department at 1-877-777-3450.

correlation to the standards (cont.)

standards correlation chart

The lessons in this guide were written to support the Common Core College and Career Readiness Anchor Standards. This chart indicates which sections of this guide address the anchor standards.

Common Core College and Career Readiness Anchor Standard	Section
CCSS.ELA-Literacy.CCRA.R.1—Read closely to determine what the text says explicitly and to make logical inferences from it; cite specific textual evidence when writing or speaking to support conclusions drawn from the text.	Analyzing the Literature Sections 1–4; Guided Close Reading Sections 1–4; Story Elements Sections 1–4
CCSS.ELA-Literacy.CCRA.R.2—Determine central ideas or themes of a text and analyze their development; summarize the key supporting details and ideas.	Analyzing the Literature Sections 1–4; Guided Close Reading Sections 1–4; Making Connections Section 4; Post-Reading Response to Literature; Culminating Activity
CCSS.ELA-Literacy.CCRA.R.3—Analyze how and why individuals, events, or ideas develop and interact over the course of a text.	Analyzing the Literature Sections 1–4; Guided Close Reading Sections 1–4; Story Elements Sections 1–4; Post-Reading Response to Literature
CCSS.ELA-Literacy.CCRA.R.4—Interpret words and phrases as they are used in a text, including determining technical, connotative, and figurative meanings, and analyze how specific word choices shape meaning or tone.	Vocabulary Sections 1–4; Making Connections Sections 1, 3
CCSS.ELA-Literacy.CCRA.R.5—Analyze the structure of texts, including how specific sentences, paragraphs, and larger portions of the text relate to each other and the whole.	Post-Reading Theme Thoughts
CCSS.ELA-Literacy.CCRA.R.7—Integrate and evaluate content presented in diverse media and formats, including visually and quantitatively, as well as in words.	Pre-Reading Activities; Story Elements Section 1
CCSS.ELA-Literacy.CCRA.R.10—Read and comprehend complex literary and informational texts independently and proficiently.	Entire Unit
CCSS.ELA-Literacy.CCRA.W.1—Write arguments to support claims in an analysis of substantive topics or texts using valid reasoning and relevant and sufficient evidence.	Reader Response Section 4

correlation to the standards (cont.)

standards correlation chart (cont.)

Common Core College and Career Readiness Anchor Standard	Section
CCSS.ELA-Literacy.CCRA.W.2—Write informative/ explanatory texts to examine and convey complex ideas and information clearly and accurately through the effective selection, organization, and analysis of content	Reader Response Section 2
CCSS.ELA-Literacy.CCRA.W.3—Write narratives to develop real or imagined experiences or events using effective technique, well-chosen details and well-structured event sequences.	Reader Response Sections 1, 3; Story Elements Section 4
CCSS.ELA-Literacy.CCRA.L.1—Demonstrate command of the conventions of standard English grammar and usage when writing or speaking.	Language Learning Sections 1, 3
CCSS.ELA-Literacy.CCRA.L.2—Demonstrate command of the conventions of standard English capitalization, punctuation, and spelling when writing.	Language Learning Sections 2, 4; Reader Response Sections 1–4; Story Elements Sections 1, 3–4
CCSS.ELA-Literacy.CCRA.L.4—Determine or clarify the meaning of unknown and multiple-meaning words and phrases by using context clues, analyzing meaningful word parts, and consulting general and specialized reference materials, as appropriate.	Vocabulary Sections 1–4
CCSS.ELA-Literacy.CCRA.L.6—Acquire and use accurately a range of general academic and domain-specific words and phrases sufficient for reading, writing, speaking, and listening at the college and career readiness level; demonstrate independence in gathering vocabulary knowledge when encountering an unknown term important to comprehension or expression.	Vocabulary Sections 1–4

TESOL and WIDA Standards

The lessons in this book promote English language development for English language learners. The following TESOL and WIDA English Language Development Standards are addressed through the activities in this book:

- **Standard 1:** English language learners communicate for social and instructional purposes within the school setting.

- **Standard 2:** English language learners communicate information, ideas, and concepts necessary for academic success in the content area of language arts.

About the Author—P.D. Eastman

Philip Dey Eastman was born on November 25, 1909, in Amherst, Massachusetts. He is better known by his pen name, P.D. Eastman. Little is known about his childhood, but it is known that he attended and graduated from Amherst College as well as the National Academy of Design in New York City. After college, Eastman moved to Los Angeles. His early career included art jobs at Walt Disney Productions and Warner Brothers. Eastman married Mary Louise Whitham in 1941.

In 1943, Eastman joined the army. His job assignment was with the Signal Corps Film unit. Theodor Seuss Geisel (later known by the pen name Dr. Seuss) was the head of the film unit, and under Geisel's direction, Eastman worked as a writer and storyboard artist for army training films.

After the army, Eastman worked at United Productions of America (UPA) as a writer and storyboard artist. He worked on the cartoon *Mr. Magoo*. Eastman also helped adapt the children's record *Gerald McBoing Boing* by Theodor Geisel into a short film.

In 1954, Eastman, his wife, and two sons moved from Los Angeles to Westport, Connecticut, where he continued his art career doing freelance work. His career in books began when Theodor Geisel asked him to write for a new series of Beginner Books for Random House.

Eastman died on January 7, 1986. Before his death, he had written or illustrated many favorite books, including: *Are You My Mother?*, *Go, Dog, Go!*, *The Best Nest*, and *Fish Out of Water*.

Possible Texts for Text Comparisons

Although *Are You My Mother?* is not a book in a series, there are several other books by P.D. Eastman with birds as characters. These books make for excellent comparisons of texts by the same author: *Flap Your Wings*, *The Best Nest*, and *My Nest Is Best* (based on *The Best Nest*).

Cross-Curricular Connection

This book can be used in a science unit about animals as students begin to understand the characteristics of birds and that animals closely resemble their parents. In social studies, this book can be used as part of a unit on families.

Book Summary of *Are You My Mother?*

Babies need someone to love them, even baby birds. P.D. Eastman tells what happens to a baby bird that cannot find his mother. In the story, a mother bird can tell that the egg she has been sitting on is about to hatch, so she goes to find food for the baby. While she is gone, the egg hatches.

The newly hatched baby bird desperately looks for his mother. As he does, he falls out of the nest and tree. He cannot fly yet, so he sets out walking to look for his mother. The baby is not wise to the world yet, so he approaches anyone and anything to try to find his mother, including a dog, a cow, and a boat. As he searches, he unknowingly passes his mother.

The baby bird finally comes to a large scooper truck, which he calls a Snort. When the baby asks the Snort if it is his mother, the Snort scoops up the baby bird and gently sets him back in his nest in the tree. The baby is safe at home. The mother bird returns with a worm, and the baby bird is happy to have his mother back with him.

Possible Texts for Text Sets

- Garelick, May. *What Makes a Bird a Bird?* Mondo Pub, 1995.
- Jenkins, Priscilla Belz. *A Nest Full of Eggs*. HarperCollins, 1995.
- Rabe, Tish. *Fine Feathered Friends: All About Birds*. Random House Books for Young Readers, 1998.
- Sill, Cathryn. *About Birds: A Guide for Children*. Peachtree Publishers, 2013.

or

- Graves, Keith. *Chicken Big*. Chronicle Books, 2014.
- Guarino, Deborah. *Is Your Mama a Llama?* Scholastic, 1997.
- Kasza, Keiko. *A Mother for Choco*. Puffin, 1996.
- Robbins, Maria Polushkin. *Mother, Mother, I Want Another*. Dragonfly Books, 2007.

Pre-Reading Theme Thoughts

Directions: Draw a picture of a happy face or a sad face. Your face should show how you feel about each statement. Then, use words to say what you think about each statement.

Statement	How Do You Feel? 😊 ☹	What Do You Think?
Mothers take care of their babies.		
Babies need their mothers.		
Adventures are always fun and exciting.		
Only bad things happen when you are scared.		

Pre-Reading Activities

Previewing the Cover

1. Display the cover of *Are You My Mother?* Read the title and the author's name. Explain that when an illustrator is not listed, it usually means the author also illustrated the book.

2. Point out the "I Can Read It All By Myself—Beginner Books" icon in the upper right-hand corner. Ask students if they can identify the character shown in the icon. You may want to share with students some background on P.D. Eastman and his connection with Dr. Seuss at this point. (See page 11 for further information.)

3. Point out the question mark in the title. Explain that the words in the title ask a question. Have students look at the illustration and discuss what they see. Ask students to predict who is asking the question and to whom it is being asked. Have students provide reasons supported by the cover illustration for the characters they name.

Previewing the Book

1. Take a picture walk through the book to allow students to look at all the illustrations. Pause at various points in the book to discuss what students have seen and to allow them to make predictions.

2. Based on the picture walk, ask students to identify if the book is fiction or nonfiction and how they know.

Making Personal Connections

1. Confirm students' predictions that the bird is asking the question in the title, and provide reasons. For example, the bird looks like he is talking because his mouth is open and the dog does not look like he is looking for anything since he is laying on the ground.

2. Explain to students that the bird is asking the question, "Are You My Mother?" because he gets separated from his mother. Ask students to tell about a time when they have been separated from their parents, for example: lost in a store, separated by a business trip, or simply apart during school hours.

3. Have students share ways they coped with being separated from their parents.

Vocabulary Overview

Key words and phrases from this section are provided below with definitions and sentences about how the words are used in the story. Introduce and discuss these important vocabulary words with students. If you think these words or other words in the story warrant more time devoted to them, there are suggestions in the introduction for other vocabulary activities (page 5).

Word	Definition	Sentence about Text
written (title page)	to create by writing words	The story is **written** by P.D. Eastman.
illustrated (title page)	created by drawing pictures	The book is **illustrated** by P.D. Eastman.
mother (pg. 3)	a female parent	The **mother** bird takes care of her egg.
bird (pg. 3)	a warm-blooded vertebrate animal with feathers and wings	The mother **bird** lays an egg.
egg (pg. 3)	a hard-shelled oval object that a baby bird is born from	The mother bird lays an **egg**.
on (pg. 3)	the position of being in contact with or supported by	The bird sits **on** the egg.
out (pg. 9)	a direction away from the center	The baby bird comes **out** of the egg.
up (pg. 12)	to move to a high position or place	The baby looks **up** to search for his mother.
down (pg. 13)	to move to a lower position or place	The baby bird falls **down** out of the tree.
away (pg. 18)	in or to another place or direction	The baby bird went **away**.

Name _____

Vocabulary Activity

Directions: Each picture shows a ball and a box. Below each picture, write the **best** word from the Word Bank that tells the location of the ball.

Word Bank

out	up	down	on

_____

- - - - - - - - - - - - - - -

_____

_____

- - - - - - - - - - - - - - -

_____

_____

- - - - - - - - - - - - - - -

_____

_____

- - - - - - - - - - - - - - -

_____

#40000—Instructional Guide: Are You My Mother?

Analyzing the Literature

Provided below are discussion questions you can use in small groups, with the whole class, or for written assignments. Each question is written at two levels so you can choose the right question for each group of students. For each question, a few key points are provided for your reference as you discuss the book with students.

Story Element	Level 1	Level 2	Key Discussion Points
Character	Who are the characters in the story?	Describe how each character is introduced in the story.	The characters are a mother bird and her newly hatched baby bird. The mother bird is introduced sitting on her egg in the nest. The baby bird is shown hatching out of the egg.
Setting	Describe the setting shown in the illustrations.	What words describe the setting?	The setting is not explicitly stated and very little background is provided in the illustrations, except for the tree, the nest in the tree, and grass. The illustrations show that the setting is clearly outdoors. The text and illustrations support that the baby bird falls out of the tree, walks, on the ground, and begins his search.
Plot	What is the first thing the baby does when he hatches?	Describe when the baby starts to look for his mother.	The baby bird asks for his mother. The baby bird does not see his mother, so he immediately begins to look all around for her. The text says he knows he has a mother, so he goes to find her.

Name _____

Reader Response

Think

In this story, the baby bird gets separated from his mother. Think about a time when you were separated from someone you love.

Narrative Writing Prompt

Write about a time you were lost or separated from someone you love. Tell about what happened.

© Shell Education

Name _____

Guided close Reading

| Closely reread the pages that describe the mother bird flying away (pages 3–7). | **Directions:** Think about these questions. In the space below, write ideas or draw pictures as you think. Be ready to share your answers. |

❶ How do you know that the mother bird knows the egg will hatch soon?

❷ What words explain why the mother leaves the egg alone?

❸ Is the mother bird a good mother or not? Use evidence to support your answer.

Name _____

Making connections—A Good Mother

Directions: Color in the words below that describe a good mother. Draw an *X* on the words that do not describe a good mother. Then, use some of the colored words to write about a good mother you know.

loving	hugging	harsh	mean
ignoring	selfless	cares for needs	caring
hating	kissing	selfish	sweet

_____

- -

_____

_____

- -

_____

_____

- -

_____

Name _____

Making connections—Science

Directions: Read about birds. Then, use the words from the Word Bank to label each bird below.

Birds are animals with feathers and wings. Most birds can fly. Birds lay eggs. The mother bird sits on the egg to keep it warm. A baby bird hatches out of the egg.

Word Bank

owl	penguin	flamingo
ostrich	hummingbird	crow

1. _____

4. _____

2. _____

5. _____

3. _____

6. _____

Name _____

Language Learning—
Nouns and Verbs

Directions: *Nouns* are words that name people, places, and things. *Verbs* are action words that show what is happening. Cut out the cards at the bottom of the page. Glue each word in the correct column to show if it is a noun or a verb.

Nouns—Naming Words	Verbs—Action Words

egg	walk	sat	jump	baby
eat	mother	look	bird	tree

Story Elements—characters

Directions: Choose the mother **OR** the baby. Draw the bird's face to show how the bird is feeling in each section described below.

Mother Bird	Baby Bird
1. when she is sitting on the nest	1. in the egg
2. when the egg starts to move	2. when he first hatches
3. when she is thinking about what the baby will need	3. when he cannot find his mother
4. when she leaves the nest	4. when he starts to look for her

1.

2.

3.

4.

Name _____

Story Elements—Setting

Directions: Draw or paint a picture of the setting. Include only details shown in the book's illustrations. Write a sentence describing the setting.

_____

_ _ _ _ _ _ _ _ _ _ _ _ _ _ _ _ _ _ _

_____

_____

_ _ _ _ _ _ _ _ _ _ _ _ _ _ _ _ _ _ _

_____

Name _____

Story Elements—Plot

Directions: Write a letter to a friend. In your letter, predict what will happen after the baby bird lands on the ground.

_____

- - - - - - - - - - - - - - - -

Dear _____ ,

_____

- - - - - - - - - - - - - - - -

_____

_____

- - - - - - - - - - - - - - - -

_____

- - - - - - - - - - - - - - - -

_____

- - - - - - - - - - - - - - - -

_____

_____

- - - - - - - - - - - - - - - -

_____

From,

_____

- - - - - - - - - - - - - - - -

_____

Vocabulary Overview

Key words and phrases from this section are provided below with definitions and sentences about how the words are used in the story. Introduce and discuss these important vocabulary words with students. If you think these words or other words in the story warrant more time devoted to them, there are suggestions in the introduction for other vocabulary activities (page 5).

Word or Phrase	Definition	Sentence about Text
fly (pg. 18)	to move through the air with wings	The baby bird tries to **fly**.
find (pg. 19)	to get someone or something you are looking for	The baby bird goes to **find** his mother.
by (pg. 20)	in the direction of	The baby bird walks **by** his mother.
kitten (pg. 22)	a young cat	The baby bird talks to the **kitten**.
did not say a thing (pg. 23)	to not speak or respond	The kitten **did not say a thing**.
went on (pg. 24)	to continue along	The baby bird **went on**.
hen (pg. 25)	a female chicken	The baby bird talks to the **hen**.
dog (pg. 28)	a mammal related to the wolf that can be a pet	The baby bird talks to the **dog**.
cow (pg. 31)	a bovine animal mostly found on a farm	The baby bird talks to the **cow**.

Name _____

Vocabulary Activity

Directions: Choose two vocabulary words. Write a sentence for each. Make sure your sentences show what the words mean.

Words from the Story

fly	find	kitten
hen	dog	cow

Word	Sentence

Directions: Answer this question.

1. After talking to each animal, the baby **went on**. Why?

_____

_ _ _ _ _ _ _ _ _ _ _ _ _ _

_____

_ _ _ _ _ _ _ _ _ _ _ _ _ _

_____

Analyzing the Literature

Provided below are discussion questions you can use in small groups, with the whole class, or for written assignments. Each question is written at two levels so you can choose the right question for each group of students. For each question, a few key points are provided for your reference as you discuss the book with students.

Story Element	Level 1	Level 2	Key Discussion Points
Character	What new characters are in this section?	Why does the baby bird talk to the different animals?	A kitten, hen, dog, and cow are introduced in this section. The baby bird asks each animal if it is his mother as the baby bird continues to search for his mother.
Setting	How do the illustrations show the setting of this section?	How do you know about the setting in this story?	The text does not explicitly state a setting and the illustrations provide limited details. The setting is outdoors, and it can be inferred that the setting is away from a city, probably the country due to the types of animals the baby bird talks to—a kitten, hen, dog, and cow.
Plot	Why does the baby bird keep searching for his mother after talking to each animal?	What evidence is there that the baby is determined to find his mother?	The baby bird continues to search for the mother, even when he cannot find her. He states, "I have to find my mother!" The capital letters in the words the second time they are stated show emphasis and his determination to find his mother.

Reader Response

Think

Think about how the baby bird walks right by his mother and does not even see or recognize her.

Informative/Explanatory Writing Prompt

Write about what birds look like. Supply some facts about how birds look and act.

_____

_____

_____

_____

_____

_____

_____

_____

_____

_____

_____

Name _____

Guided close Reading

Closely reread where the baby bird walks by his mother (pages 20–21).	**Directions:** Think about these questions. In the space below, write ideas or draw pictures as you think. Be ready to share your answers.

❶ Based on the story, why does the baby walk right by his mother?

❷ What text helps the reader understand why the baby asks other kinds of animals if they are his mother?

❸ What do the illustrations tell about the mother?

Name _____

Making connections—Look Alikes

Directions: Many baby animals look like their parents. Write or draw reasons the baby bird does not look like each animal he talks to.

kitten	hen
dog	**cow**

Name _____

Making connections—Math

Directions: The baby bird has two legs. Count how many legs there would be if there were more baby birds. Write your answer in each box.

Example:

2 _____ + 2 _____ = | 4 legs |

1. _____ + _____ + _____ = | |

2. _____ + _____ + _____ + _____ = | |

3. _____ + _____ + _____ = | |

#40000—Instructional Guide: Are You My Mother?

Language Learning—Questions

Directions: Questions are sentences that ask something. They end with question marks. Cut out the question marks at the bottom of the page and glue one at the end of each sentence. These sentences are in the book.

1. Are you my mother ☐

2. Where is she ☐

3. Where could she be ☐

4. How could I be your mother ☐

5. Did he have a mother ☐

Directions: Circle the question word at the beginning of each sentence above. Choose one of the words and write your own question.

_____

_ _

_____

_ _

_____

? | ? | ? | ? | ?

Name _____

Story Elements—Characters

Directions: The baby bird asks four animals if they are his mother. Each animal responds differently. What does each animal do or say?

kitten	
hen	
dog	
cow	

#40000—Instructional Guide: Are You My Mother?   © Shell Education

Name _____

Story Elements—Setting

Directions: Draw a picture of a setting where you would find a kitten, hen, dog, and cow. Include other animals you might find in that setting. Write a title for your picture.

_____

_ _ _ _ _ _ _ _ _ _ _ _ _ _ _ _

_____

 #40000—Instructional Guide: Are You My Mother?

Name _____

Story Elements—Plot

Directions: Draw the four animals the baby bird talks to. Put them in the correct order. Write the name of each animal on the line below each box.

1.

_____

2.

_____

3.

_____

4.

_____

#40000—Instructional Guide: Are You My Mother?

Vocabulary Overview

Key words and phrases from this section are provided below with definitions and sentences about how the words are used in the story. Introduce and discuss these important vocabulary words with students. If you think these words or other words in the story warrant more time devoted to them, there are suggestions in the introduction for other vocabulary activities (page 5).

Word or Phrase	Definition	Sentence about Text
ran (pg. 38)	moved with your legs at a speed that is faster than walking	The baby bird **ran**.
car (pg. 38)	a vehicle with four wheels used for traveling	The baby bird sees a **car**.
old (pg. 38)	not new	The car is **old**.
stop (pg. 39)	to not move after doing so before	The bird did not **stop**.
on and on (pg. 39)	to continue	The baby bird walks **on and on**.
boat (pg. 40)	vehicle used for traveling on water	The baby bird sees a **boat**.
plane (pg. 42)	vehicle with wings used for traveling in the air	The baby bird sees a **plane**.
called out (pg. 42)	spoke in a loud voice	The baby bird **called out** to his mother.
thing (pg. 44)	an object	The baby bird sees a big **thing**.

Name _____

Vocabulary Activity

Directions: Draw a picture for each vocabulary word.

car	plane
boat	a big thing

Directions: Answer this question.

1. Which **thing** in the story is **old**?

_____

_ _

_____

Analyzing the Literature

Provided below are discussion questions you can use in small groups, with the whole class, or for written assignments. Each question is written at two levels so you can choose the right question for each group of students. For each question, a few key points are provided for your reference as you discuss the book with students.

Story Element	Level 1	Level 2	Key Discussion Points
Character	How does the baby bird try to talk to the objects he comes across?	Describe the reactions of the objects the baby bird talks to.	The baby bird calls out to the boat, but the boat goes on. Then, the baby bird calls out to the big plane, but the plane goes on. The baby bird talks to the big thing and the big things says, "Snort." The objects do not talk to the baby bird because they are not alive. They just continue with their jobs because they cannot interact with the baby bird.
Setting	Describe the new settings introduced in this section.	There is more detail in the illustrations than earlier in the book. Describe what is different about what is shown.	The settings show a yard with a broken-down car, a river, the air, and a construction site. In the end, the baby bird is returned to his nest in the tree. Although the background illustrations are still sparse, there is more detail in what is shown.
Plot	Describe the other objects the baby bird comes across as he is looking for his mother.	How do the illustrations or pictures help you to find out what other objects the baby bird comes across as he is looking for his mother?	The baby bird comes across a car, a boat, a plane, and a front-loader. The boat and the plane keep moving on. The illustrations clearly show all of these vehicles. The illustrations show these vehicles in their settings and help the reader to understand what a boat, plane, and front-loader are.

Name _____

Reader Response

Think

Think about how the baby bird goes in search of his mother. He comes across many types of transportation, such as a car, a boat, and a plane.

Narrative Writing Prompt

Write about the different things you see when you are on your way to school.

_____

- -

_____

_____

- -

_____

_____

- -

_____

_____

- -

_____

Name _____

Guided close Reading

Closely reread where the baby bird first interacts with the Snort (pages 46–49).

Directions: Think about these questions. In the space below, write ideas or draw pictures as you think. Be ready to share your answers.

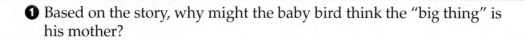

❶ Based on the story, why might the baby bird think the "big thing" is his mother?

❷ What does the "big thing" say?

❸ What evidence is there that the baby bird is afraid of the Snort?

Name _____

Making connections—
Birds and Airplanes

Directions: The baby bird is similar to an airplane. Think about all the ways birds and airplanes are the same and the ways they are different. Draw and write in this Venn diagram.

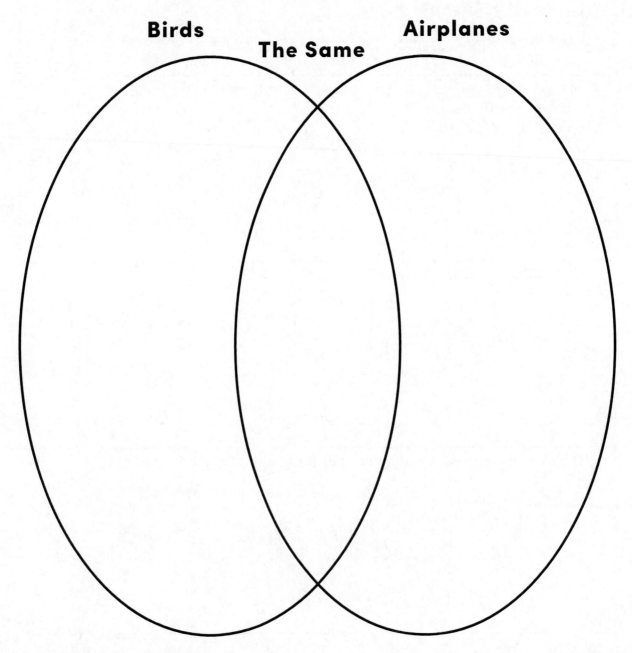

Birds   **The Same**   **Airplanes**

Name _____

Making connections—Social Studies

Directions: There are different types of transportation in this section of the story. Cut out each object below and glue it in the correct column.

Land	Water	Air

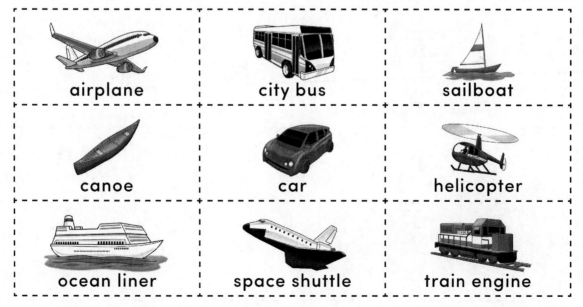

airplane | city bus | sailboat

canoe | car | helicopter

ocean liner | space shuttle | train engine

#40000—Instructional Guide: Are You My Mother?

Name _____

Language Learning—Adjectives

Directions: Adjectives describe nouns. Write some adjectives to describe these items in the book.

Object from the Story	Adjectives

#40000—Instructional Guide: Are You My Mother?

Name _____

Story Elements—characters

Directions: The big thing says, "Snort." Write what the car, boat, and plane would say if they talked.

car

boat

plane

#40000—Instructional Guide: Are You My Mother? 45

Name _____

Story Elements—Plot

Directions: Pick something else to have the baby bird talk to. Write dialogue between the baby bird and this other "mother."

" _____

_____

_____

_____ ," says the bird.

The _____ says, " _____

_____

_____ "
.

The bird says, " _____

_____ "
.

" _____

_____

_____ ," answers the _____ .

Name _____

Story Elements—Setting

Directions: Draw your favorite setting in this section of the story. Be sure to include many details in your picture.

Vocabulary Overview

Key words and phrases from this section are provided below with definitions and sentences about how the words are used in the story. Introduce and discuss these important vocabulary words with students. If you think these words or other words in the story warrant more time devoted to them, there are suggestions in the introduction for other vocabulary activities (page 5).

Word or Phrase	Definition	Sentence about Text
way up (pg. 50)	up high	The Snort went **way up**.
just then (pg. 50)	a particular time in the past	**Just then**, it came to a stop.
home (pg. 59)	the place a person or animal lives	The tree is the baby bird's **home**.
happened (pg. 59)	took place	Something **happened**.
right back (pg. 59)	in the same place	The baby bird is put **right back** in the tree.
tree (pg. 59)	a tall woody plant	The baby bird is put back into the **tree**.
came back (pg. 60)	returned	The mother bird **came back**.
know (pg. 60)	to recognize someone or something	Do you **know** who I am?

Vocabulary Activity

Directions: Complete each sentence below. Use one of the words or phrases listed.

Words and Phrases from the Story

way up	just then	home	happened
right back	tree	came back	know

1. The Snort puts the baby bird _____

   in the _____ .

2. The Snort goes _____ .

3. The baby bird is then _____ .

4. The mother bird _____

   comes back to the tree.

Directions: Answer this question.

5. What does the baby bird now **know**?

_____

— — — — — — — — — — — — — —

_____

_____

_____

Analyzing the Literature

Provided below are discussion questions you can use in small groups, with the whole class, or for written assignments. Each question is written at two levels so you can choose the right question for each group of students. For each question, a few key points are provided for your reference as you discuss the book with students.

Story Element	Level 1	Level 2	Key Discussion Points
Character	What does the baby bird say to its mother when they see each other?	Describe how the baby bird feels when he sees his mother.	The baby bird says, "I know who you are." The baby bird then goes on to say all the things the mother is not. Then, the baby bird says, "You are a bird, and you are my mother." The baby bird is very happy, and the illustrations show that.
Setting	Describe the setting shown in the illustrations.	What words describe the setting?	The setting is a field with a front-loader in the dirt and a nest in a tree. The text and illustrations support that the baby bird is helped by the Snort and put back into the nest in the tree.
Plot	How does the Snort help the baby bird?	What can you infer about why the Snort helps the baby bird?	Although the Snort is not alive, it must have a person in it to drive it. The person must have seen the baby bird and decided to help the baby bird get back into the nest in the tree.

Name _____

Reader Response

Think

The mother bird is gone from the nest when the baby hatches and then returns to her baby and the nest. Think about whether the mother bird is a good mother or not.

Opinion Writing Prompt

Write your opinion on whether you think the mother bird is a good mother or not. Be sure to supply reasons to support your opinion.

_____

- -

_____

- -

_____

- -

_____

- -

_____

- -

_____

Name _____

Guided close Reading

Closely reread when the baby bird is on top of the Snort (pages 52–57).

Directions: Think about these questions. In the space below, write ideas or draw pictures as you think. Be ready to share your answers.

❶ Use the book to tell what the baby bird wants.

❷ What words show that the baby bird is scared?

❸ Look back at the text to see what the Snort does.

Making connections—
Home Sweet Home

Directions: The baby bird is returned to his home. Draw and label the baby bird's home. Draw and label your home.

Baby Bird's Home

_____

- - - - - - - - - - - - - - - - - - - -

_____

Your Home

_____

- - - - - - - - - - - - - - - - - - - -

_____

Name _____

Making connections—Social Studies

Directions: The mother bird and baby bird are a family. Write the names of the people in your family.

mom	brother(s)
dad	sister(s)
other	

Directions: Draw a picture of your family.

Language Learning—
Alphabetical Order

Directions: The baby bird in this story finds out that many animals and things are not his mother. Rewrite the list of these things below in alphabetical order.

Words from the Section	Alphabetize
kitten	_____
hen	_____
dog	_____
plane	_____
boat	_____
cow	_____

ABCDEFGHLJKLMNOPQRSTUVWXYZ

Name _____

Story Elements—Setting

Directions: The baby bird is put back in his home—the nest. Draw a picture of the bird after he grows up and has his own baby bird. Be sure to include a tree and nest with the bird family.

#40000—Instructional Guide: Are You My Mother?

Name _____

Story Elements—Plot

Directions: Cut apart the cards below. Glue them on another piece of paper in the order of the story.

The baby bird goes up high in the big thing.

The baby bird says, "I want my mother!"

The Snort puts the baby bird in the nest.

The mother bird comes back.

Name _____

Story Elements—Characters

Directions: Write a poem about how the baby bird has changed from the beginning of the story to the end.

? ? ? Wonder

When I was in the egg, I wondered...

_____

_ _ _ _ _ _ _ _ _ _ _ _ _ _ _ _ _ _

_____ .

When I hatched, I wondered...

_____

_ _ _ _ _ _ _ _ _ _ _ _ _ _ _ _ _ _

_____ .

When I couldn't find my mom, I wondered...

_____

_ _ _ _ _ _ _ _ _ _ _ _ _ _ _ _ _ _

_____ .

When the Snort scooped me up, I wondered...

_____

_ _ _ _ _ _ _ _ _ _ _ _ _ _ _ _ _ _

_____ .

When my mom came back, I knew...

_____

_ _ _ _ _ _ _ _ _ _ _ _ _ _ _ _ _ _

_____ .

#40000—Instructional Guide: Are You My Mother?

Name _____

Post-Reading Theme Thoughts

Directions: Choose a main character from *Are You My Mother?* Pretend you are that character. Draw a picture of a happy face or a sad face to show how the character would feel about each statement. Then, use words to explain your picture.

Character I Chose _____

Statement	How Does the Character Feel? 😊 ☹	Explain Your Answer
Mothers take care of their babies.		
Babies need their mothers.		
Adventures are always fun and exciting.		
Only bad things happen when you are scared.		

Culminating Activity: Home, Sweet Home!

Recreate a nest and the baby bird with these art projects. Directions for each are provided below. Display the nests and baby birds on a bulletin board with the title *Home, Sweet Home!*

Nest Art Project

Materials

- *Nest Pattern* (page 61)
- glue
- brown scrap construction paper
- brown scrap yarn

Directions

1. Copy the *Nest Pattern* on page 61. Have students cut out the pattern.

2. Provide scrap construction paper and yarn in shades of brown. Have students cut up the construction paper and yarn into little pieces and glue them all over the nest.

Other Options

1. Allow students to go outside on the playground to gather other items from nature to glue to the nest such as grass, vines, or pieces of paper or trash they find.

2. Photocopy the *Nest Pattern* onto brown construction paper and cut out or have students color the pattern.

Bird Art Project

Materials

- 8 ½" x 12" brown construction paper (2 per student)
- scrap yellow, orange, white, and black construction paper

Directions

1. Provide each student with two pieces of brown construction paper.

2. Fold one of the pieces in half so that the construction paper now measures 8 ½" x 6".

3. Trace students' hands on the folded construction paper. Have students cut out their hands so that once cut out, they have two hand prints. These will become the birds' wings.

4. Trace each student's foot on the remaining piece of brown construction paper. Have students cut out their feet. These will become the birds' bodies.

5. Orient the footprint vertically, so the heel of the footprint is at the bottom. The head is where the ball of the foot is. Glue the wings on either side of the birds' bodies.

6. Use scrap paper to cut out two feet, two eyes, and a beak. Glue the feet, eyes, and beaks to the birds' body.

culminating Activity:
Home, Sweet Home! *(cont.)*

Directions: Copy the pattern. Use the pattern with the nest art project described on page 60.

culminating Activity: Retelling the Story

Directions: Reproduce the stick puppet patterns on pages 62–64 on tagboard or construction paper. Have students cut them along the dashed lines. To complete the stick puppets, glue each pattern to a tongue depressor or craft stick.

Follow the sequence below to practice retelling the story.

1. Emphasize with students the following attributes of a good retelling:
   - Include the names of the characters.
   - Include the setting.
   - Include the events that happen in the correct sequence.

2. Model what a good retelling sounds like for students. Use the puppets as you retell the story so students see how the puppets help you remember the characters and the sequence of events.

3. Place students with partners. Assist students in lining up their puppets in the order they will use them when retelling the story.

4. Have students practice retelling the story to their partners. Encourage students to help each other if an event needs to be included in the sequence of the retelling.

culminating Activity:
Retelling the Story *(cont.)*

Culminating Activity:
Retelling the Story *(cont.)*

Name _____

comprehension Assessment

Directions: Fill in the bubble for the best response to each question.

Section 1

1. What shows why the mother bird leaves the nest?

(A) The egg jumps out of the nest.

(B) The baby hatches.

(C) The baby bird will be hungry.

(D) She is tired of sitting.

Section 2

2. Why does the baby bird think the animals are his mother?

(A) The animals look like the baby bird.

(B) The animals are his mother.

(C) The animals talk to the baby bird.

(D) The baby bird does not know what his mother looks like.

Section 3

3. What shows how the baby bird goes to look for his mother?

(A) The boat goes on.

(B) He runs on and on.

(C) He sees a big plane.

(D) The plane goes on.

comprehension Assessment (cont.)

Section 4

4. Describe why the baby bird is looking for the mother bird.

_____

_ _ _ _ _ _ _ _ _ _ _ _ _ _ _ _ _ _ _ _

_____

_ _ _ _ _ _ _ _ _ _ _ _ _ _ _ _ _ _ _ _

_____

_ _ _ _ _ _ _ _ _ _ _ _ _ _ _ _ _ _ _ _

_____

Section 4

5. Which sentence best tells how the baby bird gets home?

(A) The baby bird flies back to the nest.

(B) The mother bird finds him.

(C) The Snort puts the baby bird in the nest.

(D) The baby bird makes a new home.

Response to Literature: Looking for Mother

Directions: The baby bird thinks many animals and things are his mother. Draw a picture of the one that you think looks the closest to his mother. Then, answer the questions on the next page about what you drew. Make sure your picture is neat and is in color.

Name _____

Response to Literature: Looking for Mother *(cont.)*

1. What animal or thing do you think most looks like the mother and why?

   _____

   _

   _____

   _

   _____

2. Is the animal or thing's response to the baby a good response?

   _____

   _

   _____

   _

   _____

3. Why could this animal or thing not be the bird's mother?

   _____

   _

   _____

   _

   _____

Name _____

Response to Literature Rubric

Directions: Use this rubric to evaluate student responses.

Great Job	Good Work	Keep Trying
☐ You answered all three questions completely. You included many details.	☐ You answered all three questions.	☐ You did not answer all three questions.
☐ Your handwriting is very neat. There are no spelling errors.	☐ Your handwriting can be neater. There are some spelling errors.	☐ Your handwriting is not very neat. There are many spelling errors.
☐ Your picture is neat and fully colored.	☐ Your picture is neat and some of it is colored.	☐ Your picture is not very neat and/or fully colored.
☐ Creativity is clear in both the picture and the writing.	☐ Creativity is clear in either the picture or the writing.	☐ There is not much creativity in either the picture or the writing.

Teacher Comments: _____

_____

_____

_____

Name _____

_____

- -

_____

- -

_____

- -

_____

- -

_____

- -

_____

- -

_____

- -

_____

- -

_____

The responses provided here are just examples of what students may answer. Many accurate responses are possible for the questions throughout this unit.

Vocabulary Activity—Section 1 (page 16)

1. up
2. out
3. on
4. down

Guided Close Reading—Section 1 (page 19)

1. "The egg jumped."
2. "He will want to eat." "I must get something for my baby bird to eat!"
3. Student answers will vary. Students may argue that the mother is a good mother because she knows her baby will be hungry and is going to get something to eat. Students may argue that the mother is not a good mother because she leaves the egg alone.

Making Connections—Section 1 (page 20)

Students' responses will vary, but the descriptors may include: loving, cares for needs, kissing, hugging, caring, selfless, and sweet.

Making Connections—Section 1 (page 21)

1. crow
2. penguin
3. ostrich
4. hummingbird
5. owl
6. flamingo

Language Learning—Section 1 (page 22)

- Nouns—egg, bird, mother, baby, tree
- Verbs—sat, jump, eat, look, walk

Vocabulary Activity—Section 2 (page 27)

The vocabulary words students choose will vary. Sentences will vary, too.

1. The baby bird continues the search for his mother.

Guided Close Reading—Section 2 (page 30)

1. The baby does not know what the mother looks like. He does not see her.
2. The baby does not know what the mother looks like.
3. The mother is getting food for the baby bird.

Making Connections—Section 2 (page 31)

Suggested answers are provided below.

- kitten—A kitten has fur and a bird does not.
- dog—A dog has four legs and a bird does not.
- hen—A hen is a different type of bird.
- cow—A cow is much larger than a bird.

Making Connections—Section 2 (page 32)

1. 4 legs
2. 8 legs
3. 10 legs
4. 6 legs

Language Learning—Section 2 (page 33)

1. Are
2. Where
3. Where
4. How
5. Did

Story Elements—Section 2 (page 34)

- kitten—just looked and looked and did not say a thing
- hen—said, "No"
- dog—said, "I am not your mother. I am a dog."
- cow—asked, "How could I be your mother?" "I am a cow."

Story Elements—Section 2 (page 35)

Students' pictures should reflect a setting that has a kitten, a hen, a dog, and a cow.

Story Elements—Section 2 (page 36)

The animals should be put in the order listed below and labeled correctly: kitten, hen, dog, and cow.

Vocabulary Activity—Section 3 (page 38)

Students' illustrations should match the vocabulary words.

1. The text says the car is **old**.

Guided Close Reading—Section 3 (page 41)

1. The baby bird does not know what his mother looks like. He asks many animals and machines if they are his mother. The baby bird also thinks the Snort is his mother.

2. The "big thing" says, "Snort."

3. The baby bird says he has to get out of there. The illustration shows a shocked face. The lines around his wings indicate panic.

Making Connections—Section 3 (page 42)
Students' answers will vary, but should show the similarities and differences of a bird and an airplane.

Making Connections—Section 3 (page 43)

Land	Water	Air
city bus	canoe	airplane
train engine	sailboat	helicopter
car	ocean liner	space shuttle

Vocabulary Activity—Section 4 (page 49)

1. The Snort puts the baby bird **right back** in the **tree**.

2. The Snort goes **way up**.

3. The baby bird is then **home**.

4. The mother bird **just then** comes back to the tree.

5. Students' answers will vary, but may include one of the following: The baby bird now **knows** his mom is not a kitten, hen, dog, cow, car, boat, plane, or the Snort. The baby bird **knows** his mother is a bird. The baby bird **knows** his mother.

Guided Close Reading—Section 4 (page 52)

1. The baby bird wants to go home. The baby bird wants his mother.

2. "Oh, oh, oh!" and "Get me out of here!" show the baby bird is scared.

3. The Snort comes to a stop.

Making Connections—Section 4 (page 53)
The baby bird's home should be a nest in a tree. Students should have drawn a picture of their own homes.

Language Learning—Section 4 (page 55)
The words in alphabetical order are:

- boat
- cow
- dog
- hen
- kitten
- plane

Story Elements—Section 4 (page 56)
Students' illustrations of the settings will vary, but should correspond to the object from the story.

Story Elements—Section 4 (page 57)

- The baby bird goes up high in the big thing.
- The baby bird says, "I want my mother!"
- The Snort puts the baby bird in the nest.
- The mother bird comes back.

Comprehension Assessment (pages 65–66)

1. C. The baby bird will be hungry.

2. D. The baby bird does not know what his mother looks like.

3. B. He runs on and on.

4. The baby bird knows he has a mother and he wants to find her.

5. C. The Snort puts the baby bird in the nest.